THE LEADERSHIP C
PRACTICE BOOK

James M. Kouzes & Barry Z. Posner
with Mark Morrow

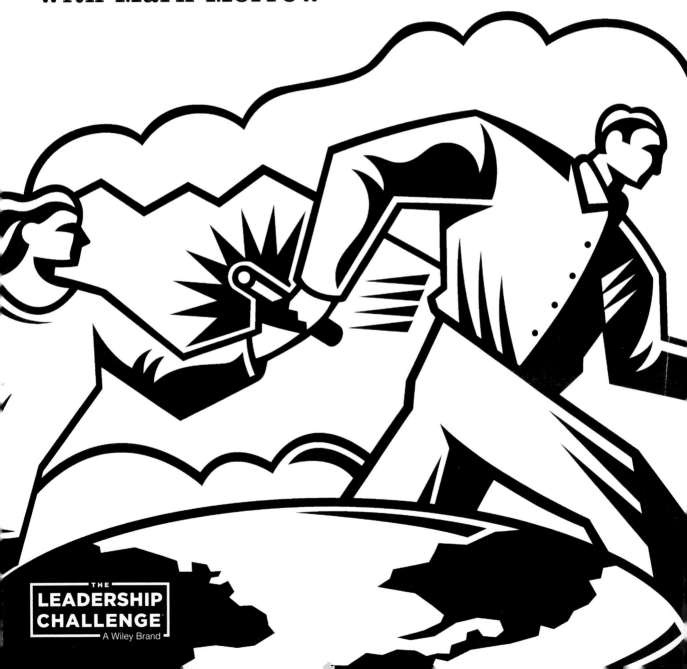

THE
LEADERSHIP
CHALLENGE
A Wiley Brand

Published by *The Leadership Challenge*®
A Wiley Brand
One Montgomery Street, Suite 1200, San Francisco, CA 94104-4594
www.leadershipchallenge.com

For additional copies or bulk purchases of this book or to learn more about *The Leadership Challenge*®, please contact us toll free at 1-866-888-5159 or by email at leadership@wiley.com.

Wiley also publishes its books in a variety of electronic formats and by print-on-demand. Some material included with standard print versions of this book may not be included in e-books or in print-on-demand. If the version of this book that you purchased references media such as a CD or DVD that was not included in your purchase, you may download this material at http://booksupport.wiley.com.

For more information about Wiley products, visit www.wiley.com.

ISBN: 978-0-470-59197-0

Acquiring Editor: Lisa Shannon
Director of Development: Kathleen Dolan Davies
Development Editor: Janis Fisher Chan
Production Editor: Dawn Kilgore

Editor: Rebecca Taff
Manufacturing Supervisor: Becky Morgan
Design: izles design

Printed in the United States of America

Printing   10 9 8 7 6 5 4

CONTENTS

Introduction

- About The Five Practices and the LPI

- How the Practice Book is structured

- How to use this book effectively

Our goal in writing *The Leadership Challenge* was to introduce a practical and accessible model to help leaders mobilize a desire in others to get extraordinary things done in organizations. Based on more than twenty-five years of research, the book is a field guide that both strengthens the abilities and uplifts the spirits of all leaders.

Embodied in the book's foundational model, The Five Practices of Exemplary Leadership®, is the notion that leadership is not an event, but a process that requires ongoing and regular practice. In this regard, *The Leadership Challenge Practice Book* provides a practical daily support tool for those who have chosen to continue their leadership journey.

THE FIVE PRACTICES OF EXEMPLARY LEADERSHIP®

As we briefly describe in *The Leadership Challenge,* leaders committing to The Five Practices of Exemplary Leadership® are required to:

- **Model the Way**—Leaders find their voice by clarifying their personal values and expressing them in a style that is authentically their own, and they set the example by aligning actions with shared values.

- **Inspire a Shared Vision**—Leaders envision the future by imagining and ennobling possibilities and enlisting others in a common vision by appealing to shared aspirations.

- **Challenge the Process**—Leaders search for opportunities by seeking innovative ways to change, grow, and improve. They also experiment and take risks by constantly generating small wins and learning from mistakes.

- **Enable Others to Act**—Leaders foster collaboration by promoting cooperative goals and building trust. They strengthen others by sharing power and discretion.

- **Encourage the Heart**—Leaders recognize contributions by showing appreciation for individual excellence. They also celebrate values and victories by creating a spirit of community.

Leaders who follow The Five Practices know how to transform values into actions, visions into realities, obstacles into innovations, separateness into solidarity, and risks into rewards.

THE *LEADERSHIP PRACTICES INVENTORY* (LPI)

Participants in The Leadership Challenge® Workshop take the *Leadership Practices Inventory* (LPI) as part of their pre-workshop activity. *The Leadership Challenge Practice Book* incorporates behaviors from the LPI into the daily practice routines and activities offered in the pages that follow. This book and the LPI questionnaire share a common goal of making leaders better by increasing the frequency with which they practice the behaviors measured by the LPI.

STRUCTURE OF THE BOOK

The Leadership Challenge Practice Book is intended to be used as a daily, ongoing practice guide for at least a year. The book's five sections follow a Monday through Friday format, with each day offering a different LPI behavior focus and supporting practice activities. Monthly and quarterly practice activities are offered at the end of each section along with a quick LPI progress checklist called Make It a Daily Habit.

HOW TO USE THIS BOOK

Since the purpose of the book is to enable leaders to regularly practice and develop leadership skills, you have complete latitude in how you approach your use of this resource. Vary your routine and approach to fit your work schedule and circumstances. However, it is important to remember that if you want to grow as a leader you must practice all of The Five Practices of Exemplary Leadership®. Try first selecting an area that you feel needs improvement; then select an area to work on that is more in your comfort zone.

For example, on Monday you may choose to complete the suggested activities for Model the Way (Section 1). On Tuesday you might choose Challenge the Process (Section 2), and on Wednesday you might choose Encourage the Heart (Section 5).

The following Monday, you may wish to start with Inspire a Shared Vision (Section 2), followed by Enable Others to Act (Section 4) on Tuesday, and Model the Way (Section 1) on Wednesday. Make *The Leadership Challenge Practice Book* work for you and push you to expand your leadership horizons.

Below is one daily routine you might choose to follow. Feel free to create your own routine that pushes you toward daily practice.

- Open the book at the beginning of each day and at the end of each day.

- Choose one of The Five Practices sections to focus on that day. Remember to challenge your comfort zone.

- Find the appropriate day of the week associated with your chosen practice section.

- Follow the simple, actionable activity instructions for the day.

- At the end of day, open the book again to review the day's activity and rate your performance of the LPI focus behavior of the day.

- In order to keep track of your practice routine and progress, complete the Make It a Daily Habit tracking sheet at the end of your chosen practice section and the Practice Tracking Matrix in Appendix A.

- Review the monthly and quarterly activities at the end of your chosen section and consider any appropriate planning needed to complete an activity.

- Repeat the same routine on the next day.

Use the same approach to complete the monthly and quarterly activities. For example, focus on the monthly Enable Others to Act (Section 4) activity one month and a Challenge the Process (Section 3) activity the next month. For quarterly activities you might choose to focus on Model the Way (Section 1) in the first quarter, and in the second quarter you might choose an Encourage the Heart (Section 5) activity.

A NOTE ABOUT LPI FOCUS BEHAVIORS

You will notice throughout the book that some days have two focus behaviors while other days have only one. Since six LPI behaviors are associated with each of The Five Practices of Exemplary Leadership®, similar behaviors were paired with a single day to match the book's five-day format. On days with two associated behaviors, you are given the option of focusing on both behaviors on that chosen day or saving an activity until the following week.

RECORDING YOUR ANSWERS

The Practice Book contains writing space, but since the intention is for you to work with the suggested activities over a year, it is more appropriate to record your answers elsewhere. Here are some options:

- **The Leadership Challenge Website.** You may go to the The Leadership Challenge website (www .leadershipchallenge.com/go/practicebook) to download recording template pages for the activities. (See page 4 for the password.)

- **Computer Document.** Create a document on your computer and record your answers in a program of your choice.

- **Online or Paper Journal.** Create a personal online journal or blog using any of the free websites (a simple Internet search should offer a number of viable options) or use a paper journal or notebook.

APPENDICES

This book includes two appendices described below.

APPENDIX A

The Practice Tracking Matrix provided in Appendix A is designed to help you track your practice routine. Note the date next to the day of your chosen practice. Over time you will build a visual representation of your progress and areas that need more attention. This matrix is also available online for download at www.leadershipchallenge.com/go/practicebook. (See page 4 for the password.)

APPENDIX B

This appendix offers basic information on how to access and use online social networking tools such as Facebook and Twitter, as well as how to use tools such as Podcasts, Blogs, and Wikis. Review this appendix if you need basic information on accessing and using these social networking tools to complete the suggested online practice activity.

MODEL THE WAY

- Clarify values by finding your voice and affirming shared values.

- Set the example by aligning actions with shared values.

PRACTICE ROUTINES

Monday*

> **The behavior that is modeled becomes the behavior that is followed.**

FOCUS LPI BEHAVIOR

A leader's visions and values are made real by direct example. It's tangible evidence that the leader is personally committed.

Review today's two LPI focus behaviors. Choose one behavior to focus on today and save the other for next Monday, or take on a more challenging assignment and focus on both today. Feel free to change your pattern of focus on successive Mondays throughout the year. Complete the associated activities that follow.

LPI ITEM #1: I set a personal example of what I expect of others.

LPI ITEM #11: I follow through on the promises and commitments I make.

TODAY'S ACTIVITY

Activity Instructions: Credible leaders must fully comprehend the deeply held beliefs that drive them and be able to communicate these values in unique and authentic ways. Focus today on setting a personal example and/or following through on commitments. Answer the following questions at the end of the day.

1: How did you demonstrate one of your key values today?

....

- -

....

- -

*To download additional recording pages for all activities, go to www.leadershipchallenge.com/go/practicebook. [User name: practice; password: kouzes]

2: What actions may have demonstrated a value you don't hold and might not want others to emulate?

....

....

Online Practice Activity*

As a leader practicing DWYSYWD behavior, create a blog that publishes both your promises and your progress toward meeting these commitments.

Activity Instructions:

Create a simple commitment blog and publish the commitments made and the progress made toward meeting them. Invite your team members or constituents to comment and participate in the ongoing posts.

3: How did you practice follow through using DWYSYWD?

....

....

4: What steps did you take to fulfill any promises made?

....

....

----

*Online practice activities adapted from Beth High's contribution to *The Challenge Continues* by James M. Kouzes, Barry Z. Posner, with Jane Bozarth.

TRACK YOUR PROGRESS

Activity Instructions: At the end of the day, rate yourself on one or both of the LPI focus behaviors of the day. Rate your performance for the day on a scale from 1 to 10 and explain why you gave yourself this rating on one or both of these behaviors.

YOUR RATING:

YOUR RATING:

LPI ITEM #1: I set a personal example of what I expect of others.

LPI ITEM #11: I follow through on the promises and commitments I make.

Why did you rate yourself this way?

....

- -

....

- -

Value Quizzes

Michael Ryan of Network Appliance held "value quizzes" in his staff meetings. He asked various team members to recall the NetApp values of "simplify the solution, trust each other, teamwork is critical, and synergy with partners." He asked team members to provide examples of these values in their daily work. "We would then comment about our current project," he recalled, "and discuss how well these values were or were not being upheld, and what to do about any misalignments."

Tuesday

FOCUS LPI BEHAVIOR

Leaders make choices about where they spend their time and attention. Your choices are the single biggest indicator to other people of what's important to you.

Review today's LPI behavior focus below. Complete the associated activities that follow to reinforce your practice of the behavior.

LPI ITEM #6: I spend time and energy making certain that the people I work with adhere to the principles and standards we have agreed on.

TODAY'S ACTIVITY

Activity Instructions: If an independent auditor were to compare the daily activities on your calendar to the values you espouse, what would the audit report reveal? Keep track of how you spend your time today. Answer the following questions at the end of the day.

1: What inconsistencies did you find between the values you espouse and how you spent your time today?

....

- -

....

- -

> You can't have the courage of your convictions if you have no convictions

2: How will you realign your actions to be more consistent with your values?

....

- -

....

- -

Online Practice Activity

A podcast is one of the most direct and accessible ways to deliver a "values message" to team members or constituents.

Activity Instructions:

Create an audio podcast as a forum to broadcast your values and to demonstrate how your values align with organizational and team values.

3: What percentage of time did you spend modeling shared values? What percentage of time did you spend being sure others adhered to shared values?

....

- -

....

- -

4: What changes can you make to improve your ratios?

....

- -

....

- -

TRACK YOUR PROGRESS

Activity Instructions: At the end of the day rate yourself on the LPI focus behavior of the day. Rate your performance for the day on a scale from 1 to 10 and explain why you gave yourself this rating.

YOUR RATING: [   ]

LPI ITEM #6: I spend time and energy making certain that the people I work with adhere to the principles and standards we have agreed on.

Why did you rate yourself this way?

....

- -

....

- -

Taking Time to Be There

Logitech's vice president of worldwide human resources, Roberta Linsky, traveled from the company's Fremont, California, headquarters to Suzhou, China, to attend Lunar New Year celebrations in the company's China manufacturing facility. Being there for the celebration in person said more about how much Roberta values her constituents than any e-mail message, telegram, card, or video could ever do.

The Leadership Challenge® Practice Book. Copyright © 2010 by James M. Kouzes and Barry Z. Posner. Reproduced by permission of Pfeiffer, an Imprint of Wiley. www.pfeiffer.com.

Wednesday

FOCUS LPI BEHAVIOR

Leaders often fear the exposure and vulnerability that come with direct and honest feedback. However, the best leaders are those who are willing to hear what's going on with others.

Review today's LPI behavior focus below. Complete the associated activities that follow to reinforce your practice of the behavior.

LPI ITEM #16: I ask for feedback on how my actions affect other people's performance.

TODAY'S ACTIVITY

Activity Instructions: Learning to be a better leader requires getting comfortable with honest dialogue and feedback. Focus on asking for feedback today and answer the following questions at the end of the day.

1: I engaged at least one team member or constituent in conversation for feedback.

....

- -

....

- -

Leadership
is a dialogue,
not a
monologue.

2: Describe the conversation and feedback you got.

....

....

3: How will this feedback improve your performance as a leader?

....

....

Online Practice Activity

Use the instant feedback of Twitter to build your feedback experience.

Activity Instructions:

Set up a Twitter account for an appropriate project or initiative. Ask your team members or constituents to report developments, react to ideas and suggestions.

4: How will it improve the performance of the team member or constituent?

....

....

TRACK YOUR PROGRESS

Activity Instructions: At the end of the day rate yourself on the LPI focus behavior of the day. Rate your performance for the day on a scale from 1 to 10 and explain why you gave yourself this rating.

YOUR RATING:

LPI ITEM #16: I ask for feedback on how my actions affect other people's performance.

Why did you rate yourself this way?

_____

. . . .

_____

. . . .

Performance Review Feedback

As vice president of AgDirect and Leasing, Farm Credit Services (FCS) of America, Troy Hansen had heard that performance reviews were a negative experience for his team members. To change that dynamic, Troy asked his team members to evaluate his performance first and to deliver the results to him face-to-face in the presence of all his team members. Although the feedback was hard to hear, Troy admitted the risk was worth the effort. His team gained a newfound respect for the performance review process, and it brought increased credibility for Troy and his leadership style.

WEDNESDAY | MODEL THE WAY | PAGE 12

Thursday

FOCUS LPI BEHAVIOR

Everything a leader does impacts his or her ability to rally the organization around a common set of values. Review today's LPI behavior focus below. Complete the associated activities that follow to reinforce your practice of the behavior.

LPI ITEM #21: I build consensus around a common set of values for running our organization.

TODAY'S ACTIVITY

Activity Instructions: A common set of values is forged not forced and is built through process and not pronouncements. Focus on taking a specific action today to build common values. Answer the following questions at the end of the day.

1: Did you take action today to become a credible, consensus-building leader?

....

- -

....

- -

For people to understand and come to agree with values, they must participate in the process; unity is forged, not forced.

The Leadership Challenge® Practice Book. Copyright © 2010 by James M. Kouzes and Barry Z. Posner. Reproduced by permission of Pfeiffer, an Imprint of Wiley. www.pfeiffer.com.

2: Describe the action and how it helped "forge" your team or constituent values.

....

- -

....

- -

Online Practice Activity

Use the personal, authentic delivery of a podcast to demonstrate commitment to shared values.

Activity Instructions:

Ask a team member or constituent to recount how a shared value was recently demonstrated and publish the audio podcast. For example, a two- to three-minute "going the extra mile" for a customer story might be highly effective.

3: List three ways you can use this consensus-building moment for greater team or constituent benefit.

....

- -

....

- -

TRACK YOUR PROGRESS

Activity Instructions: At the end of the day rate yourself on the LPI focus behavior of the day. Rate your performance for the day on a scale from 1 to 10 and explain why you gave yourself this rating.

YOUR RATING:

LPI ITEM #21: I build consensus around a common set of values for running our organization.

Why did you rate yourself this way?

....

- -

....

- -

Storytelling Benefits

Storytelling is one of the most effective ways to communicate standards within organizations. Jack Little, the CEO of The MathWorks, a Massachusetts-based developer of engineering software, confirms the power of storytelling even in unlikely environments. "Storytelling is more compelling than just giving rules, guidelines, and policies. It gives you actual examples that people can remember a lot better. Storytelling can be tied to people and names and events that are much more relevant."

Friday

The legacy you leave is the life you lead.

FOCUS LPI BEHAVIOR

Are you sending a consistent leadership message to team members and constituents? Review today's LPI behavior focus below. Complete the associated activities that follow to reinforce your practice of the behavior.

LPI ITEM #26: I am clear about my philosophy of leadership.

TODAY'S ACTIVITY

Activity Instructions: Find creative ways today to share and live your leadership philosophy. Answer the following questions at the end of the day.

1: How did you demonstrate your leadership philosophy today?

....

- -

....

- -

2: What impact do you think it had?

....

- -

....

- -

3: How might you share it with team members or constituents?

....

- -

....

- -

Online Practice Activity

A wiki offers a unique way to build and share team or constituent consensus and commitment.

Activity Instructions:

Create a wiki that outlines what you believe are the shared values of your team or constituents. Publish the wiki and have members of your team or organization create, amend, or improve the published content. Use the feedback to test your own notions of leadership clarity.

TRACK YOUR PROGRESS

Activity Instructions: At the end of the day rate your success building clarity around your leadership philosophy. Rate your performance on a scale from 1 to 10 and explain why you gave yourself this rating.

YOUR
RATING:

LPI ITEM #26: I am clear about my philosophy of leadership.

Why did you rate yourself this way?

....

- -

....

- -

The Importance of Language

At DaVita, memorable catchphrases infuse the daily conversation and reinforce the company's values and management practices. As the largest independent provider of dialysis services in the United States for patients suffering from chronic kidney failure "all the words and phrases [the company uses] evolved over time and have ended up being symbolic of the messages we are trying to send," says Joe Mello, the company's chief operating officer. "You have to make sure that everybody has a good understanding of what the beliefs are and a good understanding of what the expected behaviors are."

Make It a Daily Habit

Use this daily direct action checklist that supports Model the Way practices. Check the statements as part of your daily practice routine and note the dates in the space provided.

ACTION	DATE		

I practiced DWYSYWD today.

☐ _____ ☐ _____ ☐ _____

☐ _____ ☐ _____ ☐ _____

☐ _____ ☐ _____ ☐ _____

☐ _____ ☐ _____ ☐ _____

I set an example today by aligning actions with shared values.

☐ _____ ☐ _____ ☐ _____

☐ _____ ☐ _____ ☐ _____

☐ _____ ☐ _____ ☐ _____

☐ _____ ☐ _____ ☐ _____

My actions today contributed to my standing as a credible leader.

☐ _____ ☐ _____ ☐ _____

☐ _____ ☐ _____ ☐ _____

☐ _____ ☐ _____ ☐ _____

☐ _____ ☐ _____ ☐ _____

I rewarded or celebrated people, behaviors, and accomplishments that reinforced key values.

☐ _____ ☐ _____ ☐ _____

☐ _____ ☐ _____ ☐ _____

☐ _____ ☐ _____ ☐ _____

☐ _____ ☐ _____ ☐ _____

The Leadership Challenge® Practice Book. Copyright © 2010 by James M. Kouzes and Barry Z. Posner. Reproduced by permission of Pfeiffer, an Imprint of Wiley. www.pfeiffer.com.

Make It a Daily Habit

ACTION	DATE		

I used the power of words or stories to send the right message about values or demonstrate how someone is living out values in a memorable way.

☐ _____ ☐ _____ ☐ _____
☐ _____ ☐ _____ ☐ _____
☐ _____ ☐ _____ ☐ _____
☐ _____ ☐ _____ ☐ _____

I was particularly expressive when highlighting someone living up to high performance standards.

☐ _____ ☐ _____ ☐ _____
☐ _____ ☐ _____ ☐ _____
☐ _____ ☐ _____ ☐ _____
☐ _____ ☐ _____ ☐ _____

I talked with someone today about my values and beliefs.

☐ _____ ☐ _____ ☐ _____
☐ _____ ☐ _____ ☐ _____
☐ _____ ☐ _____ ☐ _____
☐ _____ ☐ _____ ☐ _____

MONTHLY AND QUARTERLY ACTIVITIES

Monthly Activity

KEY VALUE

DATE

Demonstrate Commitment to Key Value: Leading by example aligns actions with shared values and clarifies a leader's commitment to personal and organizational goals. For example, if you say customer service is a core personal and organizational goal, you might demonstrate that value by answering customer service phones one morning a month or by making a monthly visit to a client site.

Activity Instructions: Identify one of your key values. How can you vividly demonstrate your commitment to this core belief? Capture your ideas below and choose a date when you will practice this activity.

MON   TUE   WED   THUR   FRI

WEEK 1

WEEK 2

WEEK 3

WEEK 4

Use the next page to record your own and your team's reactions to the activity and to record ideas for activities for future months.

Notes

Quarterly Activity

CORE VALUE

TARGET DATE

Dramatic Team Activity Around Key Value: Dramatically demonstrate your commitment to a shared team or constituent value. For example, if creativity is a core value, invite everyone out to buy a few kids' games at a local toy store and set aside time to play several. Use the experience to connect lessons learned to team or constituent values.

Activity Instructions: Select a core value and plan a dramatic gesture that might demonstrate your commitment to a shared team or organizational value in this or the coming quarters. Write your ideas below. After the event, use the following Notes page to record your observations, your team's reactions, and ideas for future quarters.

Notes

INSPIRE A SHARED VISION

- Envision the future by imagining exciting and ennobling possibilities.

- Enlist others in a common vision by appealing to shared aspirations.

PRACTICE ROUTINES

Monday

FOCUS LPI BEHAVIOR

Exemplary leaders are forward-looking; they imagine the greater opportunities to come and ensure that what they see is also something that others can see.

Review today's LPI behavior focus below. Complete the associated activities that follow to reinforce your practice of the behavior.

LPI ITEM #2: I talk about future trends that will influence how our work gets done.

TODAY'S ACTIVITY

Activity Instructions: Turning possibility thinking into an inspiring vision is the leader's challenge. Focus today on communicating your vision of the future. Answer the following questions at the end of the day.

1: How did you demonstrate "possibility thinking" today?

....

- -

....

- -

All endeavors, big or small, begin in the mind's eye.

2: What new or innovative future trend idea did you discuss?

....

- -

....

- -

3: How will this trend impact your team, constituents, or organization?

....

- -

....

- -

Online Practice Activity

Podcasting is an anywhere, any time way to demonstrate your credentials as a forward-looking leader.

Activity Instructions:

Identify a key trend that you believe will impact your organization. Create and distribute an audio podcast outlining your belief about this trend or future vision.

4: List two ways you will communicate this future trends vision.

....

- -

....

- -

The Leadership Challenge® Practice Book. Copyright © 2010 by James M. Kouzes and Barry Z. Posner. Reproduced by permission of Pfeiffer, an Imprint of Wiley. www.pfeiffer.com.

TRACK YOUR PROGRESS

Activity Instructions: At the end of the day, rate yourself on the LPI focus behavior of the day. Rate your performance for the day on a scale from 1 to 10 and explain why you gave yourself this rating.

YOUR RATING:

LPI ITEM #2: I talk about future trends that will influence how our work gets done.

Why did you rate yourself this way?

....

....

Vision of HopeLab

Pam Omidyar, founder of HopeLab, knows all about visioning the future and making it happen. As a researcher in cellular immunology at Stanford University, Pam created an innovative concept called Re-Mission™ that essentially enlisted the body's natural disease-fighting enzymes to stop cancer through visualization. She got the idea while at home playing video games. "Wouldn't it be great if there were a game where kids could blast away cancer cells," she asked, "and learn about what goes on in their bodies during treatment?" Today HopeLab envisions applying the Re-Mission model to other interventions and innovations in treating obesity, sickle cell disease, autism, and major depressive disorders.

Tuesday

FOCUS LPI BEHAVIOR

Leaders are dreamers. Leaders are idealists. Leaders are possibility thinkers.

Review today's two LPI focus behaviors. Choose one behavior to focus on today and save the other for next Tuesday, or take on a more challenging assignment and focus on both today. Feel free to change your pattern of today's behavior focus throughout the year. Complete the associated activities that follow.

LPI ITEM #7: I describe a compelling image of what our future could be like.

LPI ITEM #22: I paint the "big picture" of what we aspire to accomplish.

Leaders breathe life into visions.

TODAY'S ACTIVITIES

Activity Instructions: Capture the essence of your vision in as few words as possible. Place a copy in an accessible place (your appointment book, on your office wall, desktop, etc.). Revisit and revise your statement regularly. Make any updates needed to reflect changes in the world, your organization, or your life using the following questions.

1: Has your anything happened to change your vision?

....

- -

....

- -

2: Did you share your vision today in a compelling way? What made it compelling? If you did not, why not?

....

- -

....

- -

Online Practice Activity

A blog can be a useful tool to help you hone the language and focus your vision of the future. You can also use a blog to test out "big picture" concepts that might connect to others in your organization or team.

Activity Instructions:

Create a blog accessible to your team or constituents and post the latest version of your vision statement. Invite members of your team or organization to comment and react to the post.

3: Describe what you did or said to convey your vision.

....

- -

....

- -

4: How will you deliver the vision in a more enthusiastic, articulate, optimistic, uplifting, and inspiring way?

....

- -

....

- -

TRACK YOUR PROGRESS

Activity Instructions: At the end of the day, rate yourself on one or both of the LPI focus behaviors of the day. Rate your performance for the day on a scale from 1 to 10 and explain why you gave yourself this rating on one or both of these behaviors.

YOUR RATING:	

YOUR RATING:	

LPI ITEM #7: I describe a compelling image to what our future could be like.

LPI ITEM #22: I paint the "big picture" of what we aspire to accomplish.

Why did you rate yourself this way?

. . . .

- -

. . . .

- -

Painting a Picture

Stories and metaphors bring emotional appeal to a vision. When taking over the leadership of a technology design team at Adobe Systems, Andrew Coven created a fictional company called "Code-Hawgs" (a play on words, to hog all the code) to focus attention on the team's goals and project approach. "Code-Hawgs was a systems integrator that was creating a plug-in to integrate our product with their database and workflow management system. We even created a mascot (called CodeHawg), which then appeared everywhere—on shirts, flyers, walls, etc.—to remind folks what the company was all about.

Wednesday

FOCUS LPI BEHAVIOR

Leaders are able to help people see that what they are doing is bigger than themselves and bigger, even, than revenue earned, growth rates, or returns to shareholders.

Review today's LPI behavior focus below. Complete the associated activities that follow to reinforce your practice of the behavior.

LPI ITEM #12: I appeal to others to share an exciting dream of the future.

TODAY'S ACTIVITY

Activity Instructions: Do you encourage others to share their own visions of the future? Create or access an existing list of your constituents or team members and plan to answer the following questions at the end of the day.

1: How did I reach out to learn more about the hopes, dreams, and visions of my team members?

....

- -

....

- -

Leadership is not about selling your dream; it's about creating a shared sense of destiny.

2: I identified two or three team members or constituents who were a priority and took the following actions to learn more about their visions of the future..

....

- -

....

- -

Online Practice Activity

Encourage all your team members or constituents to share their visions of the future using Twitter.

Activity Instructions:

Set up a micro-blog (Twitter) account and encourage team or constituent participation. You might offer the first Tweet describing your own vision as a way to get the conversation started.

3: Describe a recently shared vision or dream from a team member or constituent.

....

- -

....

- -

TRACK YOUR PROGRESS

Activity Instructions: At the end of the day, rate yourself on the LPI focus behavior of the day. Rate your performance on a scale from 1 to 10 and explain why you gave yourself this rating.

YOUR RATING:

LPI ITEM #12: I appeal to others to share an exciting dream of the future.

Why did you rate yourself this way?

....

- -

....

- -

A Shared Vision

Dr. Martin Luther King, Jr.'s "I Have a Dream" speech perfectly illustrates how a leader can animate a vision and encourage others to actively participate in realizing a dream. Leaders have to animate the vision and make manifest the purpose so that others can see it, hear it, taste it, touch it, feel it.

Thursday

FOCUS LPI BEHAVIOR

You can't mobilize people to willingly travel to places they don't want to go. What people really want to hear is not simply the leader's vision. They want to see themselves in the picture of the future that the leader is painting.

Review today's LPI behavior focus below. Complete the associated activities that follow to reinforce your practice of the behavior.

LPI ITEM #17: I show others how their long-term interests can be realized by enlisting in a common vision.

TODAY'S ACTIVITY

Activity Instructions: Leaders discover what constituents want for themselves by getting to know their constituents through listening and taking their advice. Focus on practicing effective listening techniques today that ensure constituents feel heard. Answer the following questions at the end of the day.

1: I took time today to listen and get to know a team member or constituent, and this is what I learned:

....

- -

....

- -

Constituents don't serve leaders; leaders serve constituents. Both serve a common purpose.

2: Briefly describe how the encounter made you feel. How did the person you listened to react?

....

- -

....

- -

Online Practice Activity

Wikis encourage the participation of others by offering the possibility of creating shared and agreed-on definitions and documents.

Activity Instructions:

Create a wiki for your team or constituents. Post a team or organization vision and offer suggestions on how the vision serves everyone's long-term interests.

3: How will you use this information to support shared visions?

....

- -

....

- -

4: How will you use the conversation to support a more open, collaborative, listening work environment?

....

- -

....

- -

TRACK YOUR PROGRESS

Activity Instructions: At the end of the day, rate yourself on the LPI focus behavior of the day . Rate your performance for the day on a scale from 1 to 10 and explain why you gave yourself this rating.

YOUR RATING:

LPI ITEM #17: I show others how their long-term interests can be realized by enlisting in a common vision.

Why did you rate yourself this way?

....

- -

....

- -

Power of Listening

Even those whose training emphasizes lead by example can benefit from listening. Jim Schwappach, a U.S. Naval Academy graduate and former submarine officer, notes that when he began to actively and deeply listen to people he got results. "I started a collaborative, open environment so as to promote the free exchange of ideas. I started meeting individually with each of them, asking questions as to what they thought were the key issues. . . . this increase in interaction allowed me to benefit from their varied perspectives and further enabled us to craft a vision that we can call our own.

Friday

FOCUS LPI BEHAVIOR

Leaders connect others to what is most meaningful in a shared vision. They lift people to higher levels of motivation and morality, and continuously reinforce that they can make a difference in the world.

Review today's LPI behavior focus below. Complete the associated activities that follow to reinforce your practice of the behavior.

LPI ITEM #27: I speak with genuine conviction about the higher meaning and purpose of our work.

TODAY'S ACTIVITY

Activity Instructions: Speak with at least one individual constituent or team member during the day about your own convictions and then answer the following questions.

1: What higher-purpose conviction did you share?

....

- -

....

- -

Leaders find the common thread that weaves the fabric of human needs into a colorful tapestry.

2: Did the team member or constituent share his or her own convictions? Briefly record what was shared.

....

- -

....

- -

3: How might you use what you learned to motivate others to a higher level of work?

Online Practice Activity

Use a podcast to share stories of conviction and purpose in work.

....

- -

....

- -

Activity Instructions:

Ask a member of your team or other constituent to share his or her convictions about work. Consider asking one of the individuals who volunteered to share during a recent conversation. Post the audio podcasts for viewing and comment.

TRACK YOUR PROGRESS

Activity Instructions: At the end of the day, rate yourself on the LPI focus behavior of the day. Rate your performance for the day on a scale from 1 to 10 and explain why you gave yourself this rating.

YOUR RATING:

LPI ITEM #27: I speak with genuine conviction about the higher meaning and purpose of our work.

Why did you rate yourself this way?

....

- -

....

- -

Create Meaning

Great leaders, like great companies and countries, create meaning and not just money. Me Chih-Chen, controller at Ravix Group, is passionate about the quality of everything she does, even when it comes to financial reports. She made sure that her staff saw why doing the work correctly and on time was connected to the success of the entire organization. Because she appealed directly to their sense of pride and self-worth, the staff performed at a higher level and understood that their work mattered and was not merely "number-crunching."

Make It a Daily Habit

Use this daily direct action checklist to support practices to Inspire a Shared Vision. Check the statements as part of your daily practice routine and note the dates in the space provided.

ACTION	DATE		
I set up a process for looking ahead and forecasting trends.	☐ _____ ☐ _____ ☐ _____ ☐ _____	☐ _____ ☐ _____ ☐ _____ ☐ _____	☐ _____ ☐ _____ ☐ _____ ☐ _____
I constantly look for ways to get input from others on their vision for the future.	☐ _____ ☐ _____ ☐ _____ ☐ _____	☐ _____ ☐ _____ ☐ _____ ☐ _____	☐ _____ ☐ _____ ☐ _____ ☐ _____
I set aside time every month with constituents to talk about the future.	☐ _____ ☐ _____ ☐ _____ ☐ _____	☐ _____ ☐ _____ ☐ _____ ☐ _____	☐ _____ ☐ _____ ☐ _____ ☐ _____
I visualize what it will be like to attain my vision.	☐ _____ ☐ _____ ☐ _____ ☐ _____	☐ _____ ☐ _____ ☐ _____ ☐ _____	☐ _____ ☐ _____ ☐ _____ ☐ _____

Make It a Daily Habit

ACTION	DATE		

I work hard to pare down and revise my vision statement to better communicate its message.

☐ _____ ☐ _____ ☐ _____
☐ _____ ☐ _____ ☐ _____
☐ _____ ☐ _____ ☐ _____
☐ _____ ☐ _____ ☐ _____

I read a recommended book to help me inspire a shared vision.

☐ _____ ☐ _____ ☐ _____
☐ _____ ☐ _____ ☐ _____
☐ _____ ☐ _____ ☐ _____
☐ _____ ☐ _____ ☐ _____

I was particularly expressive when highlighting someone living up to high performance standards.

☐ _____ ☐ _____ ☐ _____
☐ _____ ☐ _____ ☐ _____
☐ _____ ☐ _____ ☐ _____
☐ _____ ☐ _____ ☐ _____

I talked with someone today about my values and beliefs.

☐ _____ ☐ _____ ☐ _____
☐ _____ ☐ _____ ☐ _____
☐ _____ ☐ _____ ☐ _____
☐ _____ ☐ _____ ☐ _____

MONTHLY AND QUARTERLY ACTIVITIES

Monthly Activity

DISCUSSION FORUM

TARGET DATE

Discuss Future and Common Purpose: Leaders need to think a few "moves" ahead of their constituents to picture possibilities. Just as important, leaders need to understand the aspirations of constituents to build a shared vision all are committed to achieving.

Activity Instructions: Set aside time in a chosen month with your team members or constituents to discuss the future. Whether the forum is part of a staff meeting or part of a working lunch, use the time to build a sense of common purpose and connection to a higher purpose. Jot down some of your ideas to kick off the discussion below.

On the Notes page that follows, capture the discussion ideas and revisit the ideas during a subsequent forum of your choice.

MON   TUE   WED   THUR   FRI

WEEK 1

WEEK 2

WEEK 3

WEEK 4

Notes

Quarterly Activity

STORY TITLE/IDEA

DELIVERY FORUM

TARGET DATE

Create and Deliver a Vision Story: Enabling others to see into the future does not require some supernatural power. All of us possess the power to enlist others to mentally join us, whether describing a favorite vacation of dramatic life event.

Activity Instructions: Develop a story using metaphors, symbols, word pictures, positive language, and your own personal energy to enlist others in a shared vision of the future. Deliver your polished presentation at an appropriate forum such as a large staff or organizational meeting or an industry convention.

Record your thoughts for a vision story below. After delivering the story, use the following Notes page to record reactions to the story and ideas for improving or adding to the story for subsequent retellings.

Q:4   Q:1

Q:3   Q:2

Notes

CHALLENGE THE PROCESS

- Search for opportunities by seizing the initiative and by looking outward for innovative ways to improve.

- Experiment and take risks by constantly generating small wins and learning from experience.

PRACTICE ROUTINES

Monday

Instill a sense of adventure in everything you do. Instill a sense of wonder in the people who do the work.

FOCUS LPI BEHAVIOR

Are you a leader who asks why and encourages others to follow your lead?

Review today's LPI behavior focus below. Complete the associated activities that follow to reinforce your practice of the behavior.

LPI ITEM #8: I challenge people to try out new and innovative ways to do their work.

TODAY'S ACTIVITY

Activity Instructions: Use the following activity to build your questioning mindset today. Identify at least one policy or procedure used in your organization or unit or make a short list of some of the key tasks you perform, and then answer the following questions by the end of the day.

1: Why is this policy, procedure, or task used or performed?

....

- -

....

- -

2: Why am I or the organization doing it this way?

....

- -

....

- -

Online Practice Activity

Use a blog to identify tasks or procedures that need review or new thinking.

Activity Instructions:

Create a blog and give it a name such as New Thinking Journal or the Status Quo Challenge. As you discover new, innovative, or more productive ways of doing things, post the most appropriate findings and encourage others to comment or post their own ideas.

3: Can this task, policy, or procedure be done better? What purpose does it serve? Might it be eliminated?

....

- -

....

- -

4: Are your conclusions appropriate to share? If so, use the sharing to support your commitment to this behavior.

....

- -

....

- -

TRACK YOUR PROGRESS

Activity Instructions: At the end of the day, rate yourself on the LPI focus behavior of the day. Rate your performance for the day on a scale from 1 to 10 and explain why you gave yourself this rating.

YOUR RATING:

LPI ITEM #8: I challenge people to try out new and innovative ways to do their work.

Why did you rate yourself this way?

....

....

Status Quo Challenge

Arlene Blum knows first-hand the importance of challenging the status quo. As an avid mountain climber and a biophysical chemist with a Ph.D., Arlene had scaled more than three hundred mountains. However, one of her greatest challenges was leading the first all-woman team up Annapurna I, the tenth-largest mountain in the world. "We had to believe in ourselves enough to make the attempt in spite of social conventions and two hundred years of climbing history in which women were usually relegated to the sidelines," she recalled. "As women, that challenge was even greater than the mountain." On October 15, 1978, the group met the challenge to become the first American women to climb the 26,200-foot Annapurna.

Tuesday

It's not so important whether you find the challenges or they find you. What is important are the choices you make when stuff happens.

FOCUS LPI BEHAVIOR

Leaders must stay sensitive to external realities. They must go out and talk to their constituents, customers, vendors, and others who might provide insight.

Review today's LPI behavior focus below. Complete the associated activities that follow to reinforce your practice of the behavior.

LPI ITEM #13: I search outside the formal boundaries of my organization for innovative ways to do what we do.

TODAY'S ACTIVITY

Activity Instructions: Innovation requires more listening and communication. Communicate with at least one new or under-used contact today and answer the following questions at the end of the day to capture new insights.

1: What new insight did you gain from your exchange?

....

- -

....

- -

The Leadership Challenge® Practice Book. Copyright © 2010 by James M. Kouzes and Barry Z. Posner. Reproduced by permission of Pfeiffer, an Imprint of Wiley. www.pfeiffer.com.

2: How might you use or build on what you learned?

....

- -

....

- -

3: Should the contact be part of your regular network?

....

- -

....

- -

4: What is the best way to share your knowledge?

....

- -

....

- -

Online Practice Activity

Use podcasts or video links from external sources to support innovative thinking approaches.

Activity Instructions:

Use key words to search the Internet for free podcasts and videos that support new ideas or approaches to the way you currently do business. As a first step, try searching blogs using free online tools such as socialmention .com, technorati.com, and socialmeter.com.

TUESDAY | CHALLENGE THE PROCESS | PAGE 60

TRACK YOUR PROGRESS

Activity Instructions: At the end of the day, rate yourself on today's LPI focus behavior. Rate your performance for the day on a scale from 1 to 10 and explain why you gave yourself this rating.

YOUR RATING:

LPI ITEM #13: I search outside the formal boundaries of my organization for innovative ways to do what we do.

Why did you rate yourself this way?

....

....

Ingrained Outsight

Intuit, the personal and small-business financial software giant, has always relied on what it calls "customer-driven innovation." According to Jacqueline Maartense, managing director of the United Kingdom division of Intuit, this concept was the key source of company's competitive advantage. Every employee, from the CEO to the janitor, was required to spend time in "customer contact activities" from eight-hour shifts listening to customers after a product launch to in-home visits to watch customers use the software. "It was a philosophy that permeated the organization top-to-bottom," Maartense says.

Wednesday

Challenge is the opportunity for greatness.

FOCUS LPI BEHAVIOR

Making mistakes is part of the price people pay for innovation and for learning.

Review today's two LPI focus behaviors. Choose one behavior to focus on today and save the other for next Wednesday, or take on a more challenging assignment and focus on both today. Feel free to change your pattern of LPI focus throughout the year. Complete the associated activities that follow.

LPI ITEM #3: I seek out challenging opportunities that test my own skills and abilities.

LPI ITEM #28: I experiment and take risks, even when there is a chance of failure.

TODAY'S ACTIVITIES

Activity Instructions: How comfortable are you with taking risks and taking on new, difficult challenges? Remember, small wins lead to bigger wins. Examine all your current and upcoming projects and initiatives and answer the following questions at the end of the day.

1: What challenging opportunities do you see?

....

- -

....

- -

2: How might you prepare to take on these new challenges?

....

- -

....

- -

3: Do any projects offer a risk-taking opportunity? What's the risk of failure? Is it a risk you are willing to take?

....

- -

....

- -

Online Practice Activity

Build a culture of challenge and risk taking using Twitter.

Activity Instructions:

Use an existing Twitter account or set up a new one and encourage members to send Tweets that encourage innovative thinking and risk taking on current or future projects.

4: Would a small-win approach provide better organizational return than a risky big-win approach?

....

- -

....

- -

The Leadership Challenge® Practice Book. Copyright © 2010 by James M. Kouzes and Barry Z. Posner. Reproduced by permission of Pfeiffer, an Imprint of Wiley. www.pfeiffer.com.

TRACK YOUR PROGRESS

Activity Instructions: At the end of the day, rate yourself on one or both of today's LPI focus behaviors. Rate your performance for the day on a scale from 1 to 10 and explain why you gave yourself this rating on one or both of these behaviors.

YOUR RATING: ⬚

YOUR RATING: ⬚

LPI ITEM #3: I seek out challenging opportunities that test my own skills and abilities.

LPI ITEM # 28: I experiment and take risks, even when there is a chance of failure.

Why did you rate yourself this way?

....

- -

....

- -

The Challenge of Change

Sandra Stach, media manager for Safeway, uses the challenge of change to fortify her team. She challenged the validity of the media buying process and soon found supporters on the team who believed that asking questions about the status quo got better results. Although some of the suggestions were not realistic, she uses the process to "push every team member to work beyond his or her limit and to support each idea as valid and applicable."

Thursday

FOCUS LPI BEHAVIOR

Think of mistakes as a learning tool. After all, without mistakes we'd be unable to know what we can and cannot do.

Review today's LPI behavior focus below. Complete the associated activities that follow to reinforce your practice of the behavior.

LPI ITEM # 18: I ask "What can we learn?" when things don't go as expected.

TODAY'S ACTIVITY

Activity Instructions: Learning from mistakes does not have to wait until something goes wrong. Today, focus on building a mindset of learning in your daily approach to your work and projects. Ask yourself the following learning questions at the end of the day.

1: What went well today?

....

....

2: What did I learn from my success today?

....

....

> Adversity brings us face-to-face with who we really are and what we are capable of becoming.

The Leadership Challenge® Practice Book. Copyright © 2010 by James M. Kouzes and Barry Z. Posner. Reproduced by permission of Pfeiffer, an Imprint of Wiley. www.pfeiffer.com.

3: What went poorly?

....

- -

....

- -

4: What lessons can I learn from this experience?

....

- -

....

- -

Online Practice Activity

Try creating a wiki to support the idea of learning from mistakes.

Activity Instructions:

Because a wiki is a dynamic, changing webpage, use this feature to create a community of users who celebrate and learn from their mistakes.

TRACK YOUR PROGRESS

Activity Instructions: At the end of the day, rate yourself on today's LPI focus behavior. Rate your performance for the day on a scale from 1 to 10 and explain why you gave yourself this rating.

YOUR RATING:

LPI ITEM #18: I ask "What can we learn?" when things don't go as expected.

Why did you rate yourself this way?

....

- -

....

- -

Google's Celebration of Mistakes

Google is an organization that thrives on learning from mistakes. According to *Fortune* magazine senior writer Adam Lashinsky, visitors see this dynamic immediately. "This is a company thriving on the edge of chaos. . . . It's a place where failure coexists with triumph," Lashinsky writes. All engineers, in fact, are required to spend twenty minutes of their time pursuing their own ideas. Mistakes, even costly ones, are considered part of the learning process. CEO Larry Page sees mistakes this way: "If we don't have any of these mistakes, we're just not taking enough risks."

The Leadership Challenge® Practice Book. Copyright © 2010 by James M. Kouzes and Barry Z. Posner. Reproduced by permission of Pfeiffer, an Imprint of Wiley. www.pfeiffer.com.

Friday

FOCUS LPI BEHAVIOR

Leaders know they have to break down big problems into small, doable actions to build confidence for bigger wins.

Review today's LPI behavior focus below. Complete the associated activities that follow to reinforce your practice of the behavior.

LPI ITEM #23: I make certain that we set achievable goals, make concrete plans, and establish measurable milestones for the projects and programs that we work on.

TODAY'S ACTIVITIES

Activity Instructions: The longest journey begins with the first step. Are your project plans about the whole journey or about being successful each step of the way? Review your current projects or those of your constituents and choose one project to restructure into smaller steps. As part of your review process, answer the following questions about this project.

1: What are the major milestones for the project?

....

- -

....

- -

> The question is: When opportunity knocks, are you prepared to open the door?

The Leadership Challenge® Practice Book. Copyright © 2010 by James M. Kouzes and Barry Z. Posner. Reproduced by permission of Pfeiffer, an Imprint of Wiley. www.pfeiffer.com.

2: How can you break the project down into small steps?

....

- -

....

- -

3: How can you create a small-wins plan for this project?

....

- -

....

- -

4: How will you communicate your new approach?

....

- -

....

- -

Online Practice Activity

Breaking down a project into smaller, more manageable chunks is a group activity and suitable for a wiki.

Activity Instructions:

Create a wiki for a complex project and post the project plan. Invite members of the project team or group to think creatively and break the process down into smaller, achievable steps.

TRACK YOUR PROGRESS

Activity Instructions: At the end of the day, rate your progress toward creating projects that have achievable, small-win steps. Rate yourself on a scale from 1 to 10 and explain why you gave yourself this rating.

YOUR RATING:

LPI ITEM #23: I make sure that we set achievable goals, make concrete plans, and establish measurable milestones for the projects and programs that we work on.

Why did you rate yourself this way?

....

- -

....

- -

Measurable Milestones

Venkat Dokiparthi, a leader on a technical development team in India, found great power in achieving small wins. After his team reported that making a certain improvement on a product was "beyond their scope," he decided to break the task down into steps so the team could feel successful one step at a time. "I divided the task into a ten-week program," he reports, "and they actually implemented it within three days." With the encouragement of that success, the team completed the entire project in only six weeks, Dokiparthi reported.

Make It a Daily Habit

Use this daily direct action checklist to support practices that Challenge the Process. Check the statements as part of your daily practice routine and note the dates in the space provided.

ACTION	DATE		
I challenged the status quo today.	☐ _____	☐ _____	☐ _____
	☐ _____	☐ _____	☐ _____
	☐ _____	☐ _____	☐ _____
	☐ _____	☐ _____	☐ _____
I questioned the processes followed by the organization and by my constituents.	☐ _____	☐ _____	☐ _____
	☐ _____	☐ _____	☐ _____
	☐ _____	☐ _____	☐ _____
	☐ _____	☐ _____	☐ _____
I took a risk today.	☐ _____	☐ _____	☐ _____
	☐ _____	☐ _____	☐ _____
	☐ _____	☐ _____	☐ _____
	☐ _____	☐ _____	☐ _____
I made milestones achievable using a small-wins process.	☐ _____	☐ _____	☐ _____
	☐ _____	☐ _____	☐ _____
	☐ _____	☐ _____	☐ _____
	☐ _____	☐ _____	☐ _____

Make It a Daily Habit

ACTION	DATE		
I found something broken today and fixed it.	☐ _____	☐ _____	☐ _____
	☐ _____	☐ _____	☐ _____
	☐ _____	☐ _____	☐ _____
	☐ _____	☐ _____	☐ _____
I rewarded a risk-taker today.	☐ _____	☐ _____	☐ _____
	☐ _____	☐ _____	☐ _____
	☐ _____	☐ _____	☐ _____
	☐ _____	☐ _____	☐ _____

MONTHLY AND QUARTERLY ACTIVITIES

Monthly Activity

Reward Risk Taking and Innovation: Risk taking and innovation should be rewarded and the results shared.

Activity Instructions: Set aside time during a chosen month at a special meeting or regular staff meeting to reward risk-takers and innovators. Praise them. Give them prizes. Have these team members or constituents share the experience and lessons learned.

Record ideas for when to acknowledge and how to reward them below.

RISK-TAKERS TO ACKNOWLEDGE

DATE/FORUM

WEEK 1

WEEK 2

WEEK 3

WEEK 4

MON   TUE   WED   THUR   FRI

Use the next page to record your own and your team's reactions to the activity and to record ideas for activities for further months.

Notes

Quarterly Activity

DELIVERY FORUM

TARGET DATE

Innovation-Sharing Day: Innovative ideas come from many different sources. Encourage your constituents or team members to plug into these sources to mine ideas.

Activity Instructions: Create a quarterly innovation-sharing day. Have your team members and constituents share their best, most innovative ideas about improving processes, products, or approaches of your team or constituent group. The sharing can be delivered through e-mails or social networking channels such as a Facebook, Twitter, a blog, or a wiki account. Have the participants vote for the best idea and award a prize. Record the data and the delivery forum for this sharing and write any planning ideas below.

Use the next page to record your own and your team's reactions to the activity and to record ideas for activities for further quarters.

Notes

ENABLE OTHERS TO ACT

- Foster collaboration by building trust and facilitating relationships.

- Strengthen others by increasing self-determination and developing competence.

PRACTICE ROUTINES

Monday

FOCUS LPI BEHAVIOR

One of the most significant ingredients to cooperation and collaboration is a sense of interdependence. Review today's LPI behavior focus below. Complete the associated activities that follow to reinforce your practice of the behavior.

LPI ITEM #4: I develop cooperative relationships among the people I work with.

TODAY'S ACTIVITIES

Activity Instructions: Shared projects present leaders with an opportunity to promote the idea that there's more to be gained from working together than from working alone. Review your list of projects and initiatives and answer the following questions.

1: List any opportunities to involve other stakeholders in the project.

....

....

Pursuing excellence is a collaborator's game.

The Leadership Challenge® Practice Book. Copyright © 2010 by James M. Kouzes and Barry Z. Posner. Reproduced by permission of Pfeiffer, an Imprint of Wiley. www.pfeiffer.com.

2: Describe how projects or initiatives offer cross-functional or cross-organizational opportunities.

....

....

Online Practice Activity

Develop a podcast conversation between team members that focuses on the advantages and lessons learned from working together.

Activity Instructions:

Pick a recently completed project or initiative in which cooperation played a key role in its success. Ask two or more team members to participate. Publish the audio podcast and discuss it at your next team or constituent meeting.

3: Which project would be appropriate to delegate to someone else in order to foster a more cooperative relationship? To whom would you delegate it?

....

....

4: How might you involve others in future project planning or decision making?

....

....

TRACK YOUR PROGRESS

Activity Instructions: At the end of the day, rate yourself on today's LPI focus behavior. Rate your performance for the day on a scale from 1 to 10 and explain why you gave yourself this rating.

YOUR RATING:

LPI ITEM #4: I develop cooperative relationships among the people I work with.

Why did you rate yourself this way?

....

- -

....

- -

Big Picture Connections

John Doyle, the engineering manager for InfoMedia Business Unit, Parthus Technologies (Ireland), wanted team members to take ownership of their tasks and responsibilities for meeting schedules. He made sure that each team member depended on the others and that success could only be achieved through cooperation and teamwork. By informing each individual of customer feedback and financial impact of not meeting schedules, he connected all the team members to their importance to organizational success. "In the end, we were all striving toward the same common goal," he said.

Tuesday

FOCUS LPI BEHAVIOR

Sensitivity to people's need and interests through listening is a key ingredient to building trust. Review today's LPI behavior focus below. Complete the associated activities that follow to reinforce your practice of the behavior.

LPI ITEM #9: I actively listen to diverse points of view.

TODAY'S ACTIVITY

Activity Instructions: Commit to focusing on and auditing your listening behavior today. Are you building trust through listening? Do you talk more than you listen? Ask yourself the following questions at the end of the day.

1: Give at least one example of your practicing good listening behavior today.

....

- -

....

- -

The simple act of listening is a profound act of respect.

2: When responding to questions, did you use less "I" or "me" and more "we" and "our" language?

....

- -

....

- -

Online Practice Activity

Show your interest, respect, and trust for the opinions of others through a blog.

Activity Instructions:

Create a new blog or use an existing account and invite your team members or constituents to comment on a project or initiative. For example, you might describe a project with several scenarios being considered. Ask for the input of others and show your respect and trust in your comments.

3: Did you ask for the opinion of a team member or constituent? Who might think differently about a project or issue?

....

- -

....

- -

4: What did you do to ensure the team member or constituent knew you were listening?

....

- -

....

- -

TRACK YOUR PROGRESS

Activity Instructions: At the end of the day, rate yourself on today's LPI focus behavior. Did you talk less and listen more? Rate your performance for the day on a scale from 1 to 10 and explain why you gave yourself this rating.

YOUR RATING:

LPI ITEM #9: I actively listen to diverse points of view.

Why did you rate yourself this way?

....

‒ ‒

....

‒ ‒

Winning Through Listening

Brian Coughlin, managing director of Brown Brothers Harriman Fund Administration Services in Ireland, said listening made the difference when he took the job. As an outsider, he knew openness would be the only successful path. "I made a conscious effort to listen and learn from the local experts," he said. The strategy worked, and he quickly earned the respect of his new colleagues and enabled them to improve services. "We were able to mobilize people because they all had a sense of ownership and commitment."

Wednesday

Demonstrate trust in others before asking for trust from others.

FOCUS LPI BEHAVIOR

Team members and constituents who are trusted and listened to by their leaders also feel valued and respected. Review today's LPI behavior focus below. Complete the associated activities that follow to reinforce your practice of the behavior.

LPI ITEM #14: I treat others with dignity and respect.

TODAY'S ACTIVITY

Activity Instructions: Build simple, regular practices into your day that show team members or constituents that you respect and honor their contributions. Talk with at least one individual during the day in any venue—after a meeting, walking down a hall, or in your office. Ask about any support she needs, ask for an opinion on a project, or pass along information you think she needs. Answer the following questions about your interaction at the end of the day.

1: What did you learn from your conversation?

....

- -

....

- -

2: Will you need to follow up or take any other action?

....

- -

....

- -

3: In what ways do you think the interaction will build trust and mutual respect?

....

- -

....

- -

Online Practice Activity

Use Twitter to gain insight into what actions your team members or constituents feel demonstrate trust and respect.

Activity Instructions:

Set up a Twitter account or use an existing account and invite others to comment on what they feel shows trust or respect from a leader.

TRACK YOUR PROGRESS

Activity Instructions: At the end of the day, rate your progress on today's LPI focus behavior. Do team members or constituents feel more valued as a result of your actions today? Rate your performance on a scale from 1 to 10 and explain why you gave yourself this rating.

YOUR RATING:

LPI ITEM #14: I treat others with dignity and respect.

Why did you rate yourself this way?

....

- -

....

- -

Sharing Respect

To be successful in her job as Lam Research Corporation's senior program manager for the company's Customer Report Card Program, Maggie Hammid needed information to be shared. After analyzing all the customer feedback that had been collected for the previous year, she used the data to create collective goals and objectives and shared them with the reps with the message that they were in charge of their own success. In addition, she created an atmosphere that encouraged collective success and tied it all to effective sharing of information. The ultimate impact of her trust was a more successful and efficient operation.

The Leadership Challenge® Practice Book. Copyright © 2010 by James M. Kouzes and Barry Z. Posner. Reproduced by permission of Pfeiffer, an Imprint of Wiley. www.pfeiffer.com.

Thursday

FOCUS LPI BEHAVIOR

Constituents perform at higher levels and with greater initiative when they have discretion and choice in their work and support from their leaders.

Review today's two LPI focus behaviors. Choose one behavior to focus on today and save the other for next Thursday, or take on a more challenging assignment and focus on both today. Feel free to change your pattern of LPI focus throughout the year. Complete the associated activities that follow to reinforce your practice of these behaviors.

LPI ITEM #19: I support the decisions that people make on their own.

LPI ITEM #24: I give people a great deal of freedom and choice in deciding how to do their work.

TODAY'S ACTIVITY

Activity Instructions: How consistently are you providing decision-making authority and choice for your constituents? Review a list of your team members or constituents and answer the following questions and note any appropriate next action step.

1: How am I supporting my team members' exercise of independent judgment?

....

- -

....

- -

> The paradox of power is that we become most powerful when we give our power away.

2: What steps can I take to encourage creative, independent solutions to problems?

....

- -

....

- -

3: How can I provide greater freedom of decision making both inside and outside the organization?

....

- -

....

- -

Online Practice Activity

Use a wiki to foster collaboration while strengthening and empowering participants.

Activity Instructions:

Create a wiki and give your team or constituents free reign to design the workflow for a new project or process. Take the opportunity to coach and support their decisions.

4: Are there administrative changes (such as reducing approval steps, increasing signature authority, and eliminating rules) that would foster a greater sense of choice and authority?

....

- -

....

- -

TRACK YOUR PROGRESS

Activity Instructions: At the end of the day, rate yourself on today's LPI focus behavior. Did you find new ways to provide choice and support for your team members or constituents? Rate your performance for the day on a scale from 1 to 10 and explain why you gave yourself this rating on one of both of these behaviors.

YOUR RATING:

YOUR RATING:

LPI ITEM #19: I support the decisions that people make on their own.

LPI ITEM #24: I give people a great deal of freedom and choice in deciding how to do their work.

Why did you rate yourself this way?

....

- -

....

- -

Choice Improves Performance

As program manager for Intel, Grace Chan made sure people had latitude with their own choices and decisions. She empowered team members to claim ownership of various parts of a complex international project and as owners of their respective areas and held them accountable for the outcome. In the end, all stakeholders in the project were happy. "Empowering and strengthening all the members of the team to do their best," Grace said, "really motivated them to strive for optimal results."

Friday

FOCUS LPI BEHAVIOR

Strengthening others requires up-front investments in initiatives that develop people's competencies and foster their confidence. Review today's LPI behavior focus below. Complete the associated activities that follow to reinforce your practice of the behavior.

LPI ITEM #29: I ensure that people grow in their jobs by learning new skills and developing themselves.

TODAY'S ACTIVITIES

Activity Instructions: Constituents and team members have many options to help them develop new or enhance existing skills. Consider these options today in your interactions with team members and constituents. Take action to connect them to new and traditional learning opportunities by reflecting on the following questions.

1: What new skills do my team members or constituents need?

....

- -

....

- -

> Leaders make people feel like owners, not just hired hands.

2: How might these new skills or learning opportunities be provided?

....

- -

....

- -

Online Practice Activity

Creating a private social network around the topic of learning and development is a good use of this technology.

Activity Instructions:

Create a ning.com social network on the topic of learning. Give the social network an appropriate name such as The Learning Group or other name that describes the purpose. Invite team members and constituents to sign up and participate in the discussion about learning needs. The network can also provide on-the-spot informal learning for some members.

3: What other methodologies, such as e-learning, might be considered in addition to classroom training?

....

- -

....

- -

4: Is coaching or informal learning an option?

....

- -

....

- -

TRACK YOUR PROGRESS

Activity Instructions: At the end of the day, rate yourself on today's LPI focus behavior. Do team members or constituents feel more valued as a result of your actions today? Rate your performance for the day on a scale from 1 to 10 and explain why you gave yourself this rating.

YOUR RATING:

LPI ITEM #29: I ensure that people grow in their jobs by learning new skills and developing themselves.

Why did you rate yourself this way?

....

- -

....

- -

Learning Stretch

As director of product development at Vasconnect, a start-up medical device company, Gita Barry realized that building a new product would be a stretch for her and her team. To meet the challenge, she pushed her team to expand their skills and competencies. Her training push revealed a number of skills gaps that would have killed the project. "With the additional training and individual attention," she said. "individuals felt like they were part of the team and poised, even eager, to make a contribution."

Make It a Daily Habit

Use this daily direct action checklist to support practices that Enable Others to Act. Check the statements as part of your daily practice routine and note the dates in the space provided.

ACTION	DATE		
I worked on developing cooperative relationships with those in my work group, team, or other parts of the organization.	☐ _____ ☐ _____ ☐ _____ ☐ _____	☐ _____ ☐ _____ ☐ _____ ☐ _____	☐ _____ ☐ _____ ☐ _____ ☐ _____
I looked for ways to involve others in the planning and decision-making process.	☐ _____ ☐ _____ ☐ _____ ☐ _____	☐ _____ ☐ _____ ☐ _____ ☐ _____	☐ _____ ☐ _____ ☐ _____ ☐ _____
I encouraged cooperative cross-functional and organizational interaction.	☐ _____ ☐ _____ ☐ _____ ☐ _____	☐ _____ ☐ _____ ☐ _____ ☐ _____	☐ _____ ☐ _____ ☐ _____ ☐ _____
I invited a diversity of opinion and practiced active listening.	☐ _____ ☐ _____ ☐ _____ ☐ _____	☐ _____ ☐ _____ ☐ _____ ☐ _____	☐ _____ ☐ _____ ☐ _____ ☐ _____

The Leadership Challenge® Practice Book. Copyright © 2010 by James M. Kouzes and Barry Z. Posner. Reproduced by permission of Pfeiffer, an Imprint of Wiley. www.pfeiffer.com.

Make It a Daily Habit

ACTION	DATE		
I demonstrated an attitude of respect and trust of others at all times.	☐ _____ ☐ _____ ☐ _____ ☐ _____	☐ _____ ☐ _____ ☐ _____ ☐ _____	☐ _____ ☐ _____ ☐ _____ ☐ _____
I expanded people's ability to make decisions and supported the choices they make.	☐ _____ ☐ _____ ☐ _____ ☐ _____	☐ _____ ☐ _____ ☐ _____ ☐ _____	☐ _____ ☐ _____ ☐ _____ ☐ _____
I delegated work and responsibility effectively and provided the necessary support.	☐ _____ ☐ _____ ☐ _____ ☐ _____	☐ _____ ☐ _____ ☐ _____ ☐ _____	☐ _____ ☐ _____ ☐ _____ ☐ _____
I found ways to connect people and the resources they need to succeed.	☐ _____ ☐ _____ ☐ _____ ☐ _____	☐ _____ ☐ _____ ☐ _____ ☐ _____	☐ _____ ☐ _____ ☐ _____ ☐ _____

MONTHLY AND QUARTERLY ACTIVITIES

Monthly Activity

DIRECT REPORT/DATE

Coaching Dialogues: Coaching interactions are not only a way to find out what learning or skills development your team members or constituents need, but the sessions are also a way to ensure people are on track to meet performance goals.

Activity Instructions: Schedule a one-on-one dialogue with each of your direct reports and cover key questions such as: Where are *we* going? Where are *you* going? What are *you* doing well? What suggestions for improvement do you have for *yourself?* How can I help *you?* What suggestions do *you* have for me? What training or other learning opportunities would help *you?*

List your direct reports below and add target dates to have conversations with each of them this month. Use the following Notes page to make notes and to record additional topics for conversation.

	MON	TUE	WED	THUR	FRI
WEEK 1 ○					
WEEK 2 ○					
WEEK 3 ○					
WEEK 4 ○					

The Leadership Challenge® Practice Book. Copyright © 2010 by James M. Kouzes and Barry Z. Posner. Reproduced by permission of Pfeiffer, an Imprint of Wiley. www.pfeiffer.com.

Notes

Quarterly Activities

GROUP CHOSEN

VENUE CHOSEN

TARGET DATE

Cross-Functional Brown Bags: Increase opportunities for cross-functional or cross-organizational interaction to support information and cooperation between teams and departments by arranging face-to-face events.

Activity Instructions: Arrange a meeting with a group with whom you or your constituents do not normally interact. The meeting can be a brown-bag lunch in a meeting room or an informal meeting to discuss projects and discover connections.

Record the group you will meet with and the venue and target date for the meeting. Write ideas below for topics to discuss informally.

Use the next page to record your own and your team's reactions to the activity and to record ideas for activity for future quarters.

Notes

ENCOURAGE THE HEART

- Recognize contributions by showing appreciation for individual excellence.

- Celebrate values and victories by creating a spirit of community.

PRACTICE ROUTINES

Monday

It is often the simple, personal gestures that are the most powerful rewards.

FOCUS LPI BEHAVIOR

Recognition is about acknowledging good results and reinforcing positive performance. It's about shaping an environment in which everyone's contributions are noticed and appreciated.

Review today's LPI behavior focus below. Complete the associated activities that follow to reinforce your practice of the behavior.

LPI ITEM #5: I praise people for a job well done.

TODAY'S ACTIVITY

Activity Instructions: Exemplary leaders understand the importance of recognizing individual contributions. Make a point today of visiting your constituents' work areas and noting the work being done. (Make sure you have some on-the-spot validation ideas in mind.) Review a list of all your team members or constituents and consider any recent work that deserves recognition. At the end of the day, answer the following questions or take appropriate action.

1: How did you reward individuals on the spot?

....

- -

....

- -

2: What distinguished their work from that of other constituents?

....

- -

....

- -

3: How might you recognize the contribution of other individual(s) you identified?

....

- -

....

- -

4: List several creative options below beyond bonuses or incentive pay.

....

- -

....

- -

Online Practice Activity

Create excitement around "instant rewards" by using a Twitter account to broadcast the news to constituents and team members.

Activity Instructions:

Create or use an existing Twitter account. When you see high performance in action or extraordinary effort, Tweet the news to the connected social network.

TRACK YOUR PROGRESS

Activity Instructions: At the end of the day, rate yourself on today's LPI focus behavior. Rate your performance for the day on a scale from 1 to 10 and explain why you gave yourself this rating.

YOUR RATING:

LPI ITEM #5: I praise people for a job well done.

Why did you rate yourself this way?

....

- -

....

- -

It's the Thought That Counts

The cost or size of a reward is not important. It's the meaning behind it. Amanda Turner of Intuit played on a direct report's reputation as someone who approached challenges and opportunities like a "galloping horse" to provide a creative and effective reward. After a well-done presentation to the CEO of the company, Amada presented her direct report with a small stuffed horse named Victory that made galloping sounds when it was squeezed.

Tuesday

Recognition is feedback. People need to know whether they're making progress toward the goal, not simply marking time.

FOCUS LPI BEHAVIOR

Believing in others is an extraordinarily powerful force in propelling performance. Review today's LPI behavior focus below. Complete the associated activities that follow to reinforce your practice of the behavior.

LPI ITEM #10: I make it a point to let people know about my confidence in their abilities.

TODAY'S ACTIVITIES

Activity Instructions: Affirmation and appreciation increase a person's sense of self-worth, which in turns creates happier, more motivated, and more productive individuals. Pick out a few constituents and use the following questions to focus on your practice of today's LPI behavior.

1: How do you regularly show your support and confidence?

....

- -

....

- -

2: Are expectations and goals clearly defined?

....

- -

....

- -

3: Did you provide direct and consistent feedback on progress toward meeting goals?

....

- -

....

- -

4: How might you push constituents to engage their goals for better performance?

....

- -

....

- -

Online Practice Activity

Use a wiki format to celebrate and affirm individual achievement and competence.

Activity Instructions:

Create a new wiki and post recent achievements or celebrate well-executed projects. Using this format lets others participate in defining the significance and also builds a community of shared values.

TRACK YOUR PROGRESS

Activity Instructions: At the end of the day, rate yourself on today's LPI focus behavior. Did actions you took boost the confidence of your constituents and team members? Rate yourself on a scale from 1 to 10 and explain why you gave yourself this rating.

YOUR RATING:

LPI ITEM #10: I make it a point to let people know about my confidence in their abilities.

Why did you rate yourself this way?

....

....

Appreciation Basics

Team members feel appreciated when their names are included in presentations about projects, says Jason Cha. When he was challenged to reduce costs in the global industrial and commercial business unit of Tyco Electronics, Jason found that direct public recognition increased individual commitment to excellence and created a sense of community on his team. "The winner's attitude truly is one that is cultivated through meaningful feedback," he said. "It even works its magic by making me a better leader."

Wednesday

FOCUS LPI BEHAVIOR

Public celebrations of accomplishment build commitment because they make people's actions visible to their peers. Review today's LPI behavior focus below. Complete the associated activities that follow to reinforce your practice of the behavior.

LPI ITEM #20: I publicly recognize people who exemplify commitment to shared values.

TODAY'S ACTIVITIES

Activity Instructions: Recognizing the contribution of individual constituents takes energy and planning. Answer the following questions and take appropriate action.

1: What recent team member or constituent contribution deserves special recognition?

....

- -

....

- -

2: How might this contribution be celebrated publically?

....

- -

....

- -

It is not what gets rewarded that gets done; it's what is rewarding that gets done.

3: What shared value is supported by the contribution?

....

- -

....

- -

4: How can you involve others in planning and executing the public recognition?

....

- -

....

- -

Online Practice Activity

Create a ning.com account to build a social network around individuals deserving special recognition.

Activity Instructions:

Create a new ning.com network specifically for celebrating individual contributions and invite your constituents to post stories, photos, or videos that help tell the story of the contribution.

TRACK YOUR PROGRESS

Activity Instructions: At the end of the day, rate yourself on today's LPI focus behavior. Rate yourself on a scale from 1 to 10 and explain why you gave yourself this rating.

YOUR RATING:

LPI ITEM #20: I publicly recognize people who exemplify commitment to shared values.

Why did you rate yourself this way?

....

....

Big Signs

Mark Delucia, global account manager at Agilent Technologies, put out a 3-by-8-foot hard copy of project milestones for an important account and highlighted the commitments that were on time and the names associated with them. He said that once a month the team would review the data and vote on the most important team member and award him or her a gift certificate. The effort was not dramatic, but was successful. "We were able to get everyone focused on what we individually and collectively needed to do," he noted.

Thursday

FOCUS LPI BEHAVIOR

Exemplary leaders know that promoting a culture of celebration fuels a sense of unity and mission. Review today's LPI behavior focus below. Complete the associated activities that follow to reinforce your practice of the behavior.

LPI ITEM #25: I find ways to celebrate accomplishments.

TODAY'S ACTIVITY

Activity Instructions: Answer the following questions to audit your commitment to this LPI behavior.

1: Have you consistently celebrated accomplishments recently? If not, what has stopped you? How can you overcome that obstacle?

....

....

Celebrations are much more than parties; they're ceremonies and rituals that create meaning.

2: Describe a recent accomplishment you celebrated. How did your team respond?

....

- -

....

- -

3: Are you planning a celebration? If not, think of an accomplishment to celebrate.

....

- -

....

- -

Online Practice Activity

Create a celebration blog that recognizes high individual and team performance

Activity Instructions:

Create a "Great Work!" or "Go Team" blog and invite your team members or constituents to participate with you as excellent work is celebrated.

4: Describe your plans and reason for the celebration.

....

- -

....

- -

TRACK YOUR PROGRESS

Activity Instructions: At the end of the day, rate yourself on today's LPI focus behavior. What did your celebration audit reveal? Rate your performance for the day on a scale from 1 to 10 and explain why you gave yourself this rating.

YOUR RATING:

LPI ITEM #25: I find ways to celebrate accomplishments.

Why did you rate yourself this way?

....

- -

....

- -

Oscar Ceremony

Jennifer Ernst, director of business development at Palo Alto Research Center, says celebrations play a critical role at her company. For example, at one annual recognition event, the company handed out awards in a large auditorium using an Oscar Awards theme and all the associated glamour and pageantry. For each award, senior managers told rich and personal stories before calling the "winners" to the stage. Special music was played for the walk to the stage and a video celebrated the accomplishment. "By the end of the one-hour event," Jennifer said," the room was on fire, creating a buzz that lasted for weeks."

The Leadership Challenge® Practice Book. Copyright © 2010 by James M. Kouzes and Barry Z. Posner. Reproduced by permission of Pfeiffer, an Imprint of Wiley. www.pfeiffer.com.

Friday

Caring is at the heart of leadership. Without caring, leadership has no soul.

FOCUS LPI BEHAVIOR

Exemplary leaders not only reward and celebrate extraordinary performance, but they also encourage social interaction and show they care through their own personal and emotional investment.

Review today's two LPI focus behaviors. Choose one behavior to focus on today and save the other for next Friday, or take on a more challenging assignment and focus on both today. Feel free to change your pattern of LPI focus throughout the year. Complete the associated activities that follow to reinforce your practice of these behaviors.

LPI ITEM #15: I make sure that people are creatively rewarded for their contributions to the success of our projects.

LPI ITEM #30: I give members of the team lots of appreciation and support for their contributions.

TODAY'S ACTIVITY

Activity Instructions: Leadership is about relationships. Leaders must be personally involved; without personal involvement, rewarding or celebrating success has little impact. Think about the following questions during your interactions with team members or constituents today and record your observations at the end of the day.

1: How do you show that you are emotionally invested when you reward or show appreciation for a contribution?

....

- -

....

- -

2: How did you ensure that the team member or constituent knew how much you cared?

....

- -

....

- -

3: Did you perpetuate the impact of an accomplishment using a story?

....

- -

....

- -

4: How did you promote the idea of having fun on the job?

....

- -

....

- -

Online Practice Activity

Use Twitter to support a fun atmosphere in addition to "instant" on-the-spot rewards.

Activity Instructions:

Use your Twitter account and invite team members or constituents to share something funny or interesting that will make other team members or constituents smile. Post a funny picture; describe a humorous incident that happened.

TRACK YOUR PROGRESS

Activity Instructions: At the end of the day, rate yourself on today's LPI focus behavior(s). Rate your performance on a scale from 1 to 10 and explain why you gave yourself this rating.

YOUR RATING:

LPI ITEM #15: I make sure that people are creatively rewarded for their contributions to the success of our projects.

YOUR RATING:

LPI ITEM #30: I give members of the team lots of appreciation and support for their contributions.

Why did you rate yourself this way?

....

- -

....

- -

Have Some Fun

Having fun that sustains productivity doesn't have to be expensive or elaborate. Doug Podzilni, president of Gourmet Source Food Broker, simply brought a box of candy suckers to the office and placed them in the common area. In no time at all, "everyone had a sucker sticking out of his or her mouth and a smile on his or her face," he said. Later, at a particularly difficult meeting, he put another box of suckers in the middle of the table. Everyone reached for a favorite flavor and the meeting took on a friendlier tone. "It's hard to be too combative or in a bad mood when you and everyone around you has a sucker in his mouth!" he noted.

Make It a Daily Habit

Use this daily direct action checklist to support practices that Encourage the Heart. Check the statements as part of your daily practice routine and note the dates in the space provided.

ACTION	DATE		
I walked around the office today and rewarded a good job on the spot.	☐ _____	☐ _____	☐ _____
	☐ _____	☐ _____	☐ _____
	☐ _____	☐ _____	☐ _____
	☐ _____	☐ _____	☐ _____
I identified one of my constituents for praise and reward.	☐ _____	☐ _____	☐ _____
	☐ _____	☐ _____	☐ _____
	☐ _____	☐ _____	☐ _____
	☐ _____	☐ _____	☐ _____
I told a public story that highlighted high performance.	☐ _____	☐ _____	☐ _____
	☐ _____	☐ _____	☐ _____
	☐ _____	☐ _____	☐ _____
	☐ _____	☐ _____	☐ _____
I Encouraged the Heart at a regular meeting.	☐ _____	☐ _____	☐ _____
	☐ _____	☐ _____	☐ _____
	☐ _____	☐ _____	☐ _____
	☐ _____	☐ _____	☐ _____

The Leadership Challenge® Practice Book. Copyright © 2010 by James M. Kouzes and Barry Z. Posner. Reproduced by permission of Pfeiffer, an Imprint of Wiley. www.pfeiffer.com.

Make It a Daily Habit

ACTION	DATE		

I wrote a "thank you" note today.

☐ _____   ☐ _____   ☐ _____
☐ _____   ☐ _____   ☐ _____
☐ _____   ☐ _____   ☐ _____
☐ _____   ☐ _____   ☐ _____

I provided specific, positive feedback.

☐ _____   ☐ _____   ☐ _____
☐ _____   ☐ _____   ☐ _____
☐ _____   ☐ _____   ☐ _____
☐ _____   ☐ _____   ☐ _____

I asked for coaching today to improve my Encourage the Heart behaviors.

☐ _____   ☐ _____   ☐ _____
☐ _____   ☐ _____   ☐ _____
☐ _____   ☐ _____   ☐ _____
☐ _____   ☐ _____   ☐ _____

The Leadership Challenge® Practice Book. Copyright © 2010 by James M. Kouzes and Barry Z. Posner. Reproduced by permission of Pfeiffer, an Imprint of Wiley. www.pfeiffer.com.

MONTHLY AND QUARTERLY ACTIVITIES

Monthly Activity

RECIPIENT/DATE

Thank You Notes: Recognize accomplishments with a simple "thank you" note.

Activity Instructions: "Thank you" notes are personal and meaningful ways to connect with and reward team members and constituents for a well-done job. Commit to write at least five notes this month. Record the selected recipients and target dates for sending the notes. Below, record the accomplishment of each recipient you recognize.

Use the next page to record your own and your team's reactions to the activity and to record ideas for activities for further months.

Notes

Quarterly Activity

CELEBRATION CHOSEN

TARGET DATE

Celebrate: Schedule a celebration every quarter throughout the year.

Activity Instructions: Good leaders use every opportunity to celebrate values and victories, or to just have fun. Whether it's an elaborate staged celebration or a small informal team-building celebration, the results are the same.

Select the type of celebration you will hold and the target date. Record ideas for the celebration and what to celebrate below.

Use the next page to record your own and your team's reactions to the celebration and to record ideas for future quarterly celebrations.

Notes

Practice Tracking Matrix

Section	Date	Date	Date	Date	Date	Date	Date	Date	Date	Date	Date	Date	Date	Date
Section 1: Model the Way														
Monday Activity: Personal Example/Follow-Through														
Tuesday Activity: Time, Energy to Ensure Standard and Principle Adherence														
Wednesday Activity: Feedback, How Actions Impact People's Performance														
Thursday Activity: I build consensus around a common company values.														
Friday Activity: I am clear about my philosophy of leadership.														
Monthly Activity														
Quarterly Activity														
Section 2: Inspire a Shared Vision														
Monday Activity: I talk about future trends that will influence our work.														
Tuesday Activity: Compelling Future Images/Paint "Big Picture" Aspirations														
Wednesday Activity: I appeal to others/share exciting dream of the future.														
Thursday Activity: I show long-term interests, common vision relationship.														
Friday Activity: Genuine conviction of work's higher meaning and purpose														
Monthly Activity														
Quarterly Activity														
Section 3: Challenge the Process														
Monday Activity: I challenge people to be innovative in their work.														
Tuesday Activity: I search outside company boundaries for innovative ideas.														
Wednesday Activity: I seek to test my skills, abilities/take risks, experiment.														
Thursday Activity: I ask "What can we learn?" when things go wrong.														
Friday Activity: I set achievable goals, measurable milestones for the project.														
Monthly Activity														
Quarterly Activity														

Section 4: Enable Others to Act

Monday Activity: I develop cooperative relationships.

Tuesday Activity: I actively listen to diverse points of view.

Wednesday Activity: I treat others with dignity and respect.

Thursday Activity: I support decisions of others, give choice, freedom in work.

Friday Activity: I ensure growth in jobs through learning and development.

Monthly Activity

Quarterly Activity

Section 5: Encourage the Heart

Monday Activity: I praise people for a job well done.

Tuesday Activity: I let people know about my confidence in their abilities.

Wednesday Activity: I recognize those who show shared value commitment.

Thursday Activity: I find ways to celebrate accomplishments.

Friday Activity: I reward creatively and support contributions of others.

Monthly Activity

Quarterly Activity

Social Networking*

WHAT IS SOCIAL NETWORKING?

Social networking refers to a whole range of online technologies that allow groups of people with similar interests to build virtual communities to communicate, share information, collaborate, and work creatively. Social networking includes a wide range of applications from emails and instant messaging to popular services such as Facebook, Twitter, and LinkedIn. In addition, the term covers the dozens of other online social collaboration and connection tools, including blogs and podcasts as well as other applications outlined in this appendix.

INTRODUCTION

For the most part, accessing and using social networking tools is simple. Just open an Internet browser (Explorer, Foxfire, Mozilla, Chrome, etc.), type in the web address (www.Facebook.com, www.Twitter.com, www.ning.com), connect to the site, and follow the online instructions to create an account. That's step 1. Step 2, using your new social networking account, may present challenges for new users, but the learning curve is reasonably short.

The online activities offered in this book acknowledge both this ease of access and the near ubiquitous reach of social networking technology—at the time of writing, Facebook has more than three hundred and fifty million users, and Twitter is predicted to have seventy-five million individual accounts. Yet assuming a universal comfort level with these

*Material from this appendix was adapted from *The Challenge Continues* by James M. Kouzes and Barry Z. Posner, with Jane Bozarth.

and other online social networking tools risks leaving some users behind. While some users of this Practice Book will have the technical expertise, resources, and time to create a podcast or effectively use a wiki or blog, it is likely that the majority of users will be missing at least one of these key tools for success.

PURPOSE OF THIS APPENDIX

The purpose of this appendix is to close any social networking knowledge gaps by providing basic definitions—what it is and how it is used—along with a few useful tips. It is not intended to be a complete resource but rather a tool to help you bridge the gap between a real interest in using these cutting-edge tools and the reality of succeeding in your demanding job.

If you are unsure about trying one of the online collaboration tools offered in the book, try thinking of social networking as just another way to build your leadership skills. After all, if innovation, collaboration, and inclusion are hallmarks of a great leader, then surely social networking is a powerful tool to strengthen and reinforce the principles and behaviors you are trying to model.

A WORD OF WARNING

Social networking technology offers a dizzying array of choices. Try not to get caught up in the "that's really cool!" factor. You (or the person you assign to help you set up a social networking account) need to stick to the basic use of the technology as suggested in this book. After you are comfortable with the technology and available feature, then branch out and explore the "wow" factor.

Podcast

What Is a Podcast?

A podcast is a digital file of audio or video information available to watch or listen to on demand, wherever or whenever you choose. Podcasts are distributed over the Internet and watched either on a personal computer or an Apple iPod or any other MP3 player.

How to Create Podcasts

Creating an audio basic podcast is not as difficult as you might assume. In fact, it is simple to create the kind of audio podcasts suggested in this book. Simply open your favorite search engine (Google, Yahoo, Bing) and type in *How to Create a Podcast*. That's it. Dozens of free guides are available, along with more sophisticated help and applications for a fee. To get started you need a microphone (nothing too sophisticated) and the ability to record and save an audio file (.mp3) on your computer. Next, you need some basic knowledge about creating and uploading an RSS (Real Simple Syndication) file—explained as part of any "how to" discussion on the Internet and not that difficult an assignment. Once created, your audience (in this case your team or constituents) can download and listen to your podcast using a variety of methods including the use of podcatcher software that "catches" specific podcasts designated by the user and downloads them automatically to a chosen player.

Blog

A blog is a type of website. The term was created by combining the terms "web" and "log." Blogs are characterized by ongoing, regularly updated content that is maintained by an individual who "posts" commentary on events, opinions, and/or other commentary. Blogs can include graphics, photographs, or video files as part of the post and are displayed from the most recent post or in reverse chronological order. The term blog has worked its way into the language so that "blog" is often used as a verb that describes the action of adding content to a blog site.

Many blogs provide commentary or news on a particular subject or topic. Some blogs focus on a particular area such as fashion, politics, or travel. Other blogs are more like personal diaries that include photographs or links to other supporting websites. Organizations may create blogs to enhance internal communications or for external purposes such as marketing or public relations. These are referred to as corporate blogs. According to a recent report by Technorati, a social media research and aggregation site, the number of blogs is currently around 133 million active users.

Microblogs (Twitter)

Microblogging is a form of blogging that relies on short 140 character (or fewer) messages (called Tweets) to communicate with other Twitter members. Members may choose to "follow" the activities of other Twitter members on a minute-to-minute basis between blog posts and e-mail. Currently, more than eighteen million individuals have Twitter accounts, with that number expected to grow to twenty-six million by the end of 2010. The Tweets are typically sent via a computer, but can also be sent and received using a cell phone and instant messaging. Users may also send photos or audio clips or links to other websites.

The content posted on Twitter differs from a traditional blog since the entire entry may be a single sentence or part of a sentence. The user might include a photo or a short, ten- or fifteen-second video. Twitter posts range from the mundane such as what the user is doing ("going to grocery store to pick up margarine") or focus on a business topic such as leadership or management tips.

Wikis

A wiki (an Hawaiian word for "fast") is an easy-to-create website used to organize and coordinate a group's input. Users can create as many interlinked web pages as needed for the purposes of the group. For example, a group may use a wiki to gather information in order to make a decision. Each member of the group has the ability to create new pages and links on the site to hold critical information or explain or expand on concepts. Wikis are also used to plan agendas for important meetings or even to launch a new product that uses wiki software, allowing the easy creation and editing of any number of interlinked web pages, using a simplified markup language or a WYSIWYG text editor, within the browser. Wikis are often used to create collaborative websites, to power community websites, for personal note-taking, in corporate intranets, and in knowledge management systems. One of the best examples of a wiki is the online collaborative resource known as Wikipedia.

Social Networking Sites

Social networking sites are web-based services that allow individuals to (1) create a public or semipublic profile within a bounded system, (2) articulate a list of other users with whom they share a connection, and (3) view and traverse their lists of connections and those made by others within the system. Social networks play a significant role in how people connect on the Internet, and great potential exists to use them in leadership development.

Facebook and MySpace are the two largest and most popular social networking sites. Combined, the two sites boast more than 450 million users worldwide. The sophisticated social networking software created by these services allows members to create personal websites that detail every aspect of their lives from personal to professional, along with supporting photos and videos. "Friends" are added to these personal networks by direct invitation from the Facebook or MySpace page owner—a "friend" request—or by direct request from someone external to the individual's social network. Members may also join other school or workplace or regional networks.

Facebook was founded by four Harvard University students in 2006. The website's membership was initially limited to Harvard students. As the popularity grew, other Boston area schools were added to the network and it soon expanded to include an ever-increasing group of college and high school students.

MySpace is a social networking website with one hundred million users. Launched in 2004, the site skyrocketed to success and by 2006 was the most popular social networking site in the United States, although Facebook is now the top social networking site. The company is owned by Fox Interactive Media, a subsidiary of the News Corporation.

LinkedIn is a social networking business site with fifty million users in over two hundred counties. LinkedIn was officially founded in 2003 when the five founders invited about 350 of their most important contacts to join. At the end of the first month in operation, LinkedIn had a total of 4,500 members in the network.

The service mirrors the social networking capabilities of Facebook and MySpace, allowing members to post current status updates, invite colleagues to join professional networks, and create other social networking groups that share a common interest, such as a sales professional group or publishing group.

Ning was founded in October 2004 by Gina Bianchini and Marc Andreessen and competes with social sites like MySpace and Facebook by appealing to people interested in designing personalized websites around a topic of their choosing.

Ning is an easy-to-use social platform that allows people to join and create their own Ning Networks. The service has forty million registered users with more than 1.9 million Ning Networks created. The platform allows anyone to create his or her own social network on any topic or interest. For example, you will find Ning websites dedicated to running or other sporting pursuits. Ning users have also created sites dedicated to entrepreneurial women or other general business interests such as starting a business. Businesses and colleges also use Ning websites to allow new students or employees access to information about their new places of employment or schools, as well as an opportunity to meet new people virtually. Ning users also add Facebook, MySpace, and Twitter capability to the their websites to add new functionality.

Ning offers both free and paid options for users. The free option includes paid advertising that the user cannot control. The paid option allows the user to choose whether or not the advertisement is displayed.

About the Authors

Jim Kouzes and Barry Posner are co-authors of the award-winning and best-selling book, *The Leadership Challenge*. This book was selected as one of the Top 10 books on leadership of all time (according to *The 100 Best Business Books of All Time*), won the James A. Hamilton Hospital Administrators' Book-of-the-Year Award and the Critics' Choice Award from the nation's book review editors, was a *BusinessWeek* best-seller, and has sold over 1.8 million copies in more than twenty languages. Jim and Barry have co-authored more than a dozen other leadership books, including *A Leader's Legacy*—selected by *Soundview Executive Book Summaries* as one of the top thirty books of the year—*Credibility: How Leaders Gain It and Lose It, Why People Demand It*—chosen by *Industry Week* as one of its year's five best management books—*Encouraging the Heart, The Student Leadership Challenge,* and *The Academic Administrator's Guide to Exemplary Leadership.* They also developed the highly acclaimed *Leadership Practices Inventory* (LPI), a 360-degree questionnaire for assessing leadership behavior, which is one of the most widely used leadership assessment instruments in the world. More than four hundred doctoral dissertations and academic research projects have been based on the Five Practices of Exemplary Leadership model.

Among the honors and awards that Jim and Barry have received are the American Society for Training and Development's (ASTD) highest award for their Distinguished Contribution to Workplace Learning and Performance; Management/Leadership Educators of the Year by the International Management Council (this honor puts them in the company of Ken Blanchard, Stephen Covey, Peter Drucker, Edward Deming, Frances Hesselbein, Lee Iacocca, Rosabeth Moss Kanter, Norman Vincent Peale, and Tom Peters, who are all past recipients of the award); and named among the Top 50 Leadership Coaches in the nation (according to *Coaching for Leadership*).

Jim and Barry are frequent conference speakers, and each has conducted leadership development programs for hundreds of organizations, including Apple, Applied Materials, ARCO, AT&T, Australia Post, Bank of America, Bose, Charles Schwab, Cisco Systems, Community Leadership Association, Conference Board of Canada, Consumers Energy, Dell Computer, Deloitte Touche, Dorothy Wylie Nursing Leadership Institute, Egon Zehnder International, Federal Express, Gymboree, Hewlett-Packard, IBM, Jobs DR-Singapore, Johnson & Johnson, Kaiser Foundation Health Plans and Hospitals, L. L. Bean, Lawrence Livermore National Labs, Lucile Packard Children's Hospital, Merck, Mervyn's, Motorola, NetApp, Northrop Grumman, Roche Bioscience, Siemens, Standard Aero, Sun Microsystems, 3M, Toyota, the U.S. Postal Service, United Way, USAA, Verizon, VISA, and The Walt Disney Company.

Jim Kouzes is the Dean's Executive Professor of Leadership, Leavey School of Business, at Santa Clara University. Not only is he a highly regarded leadership scholar and an experienced executive, but *The Wall Street Journal* has cited him as one of the twelve best executive educators in the United States. In 2006 Jim was presented with the Golden Gavel, the highest honor awarded by Toastmasters International. Jim served as president, CEO, and chairman of the Tom Peters Company from 1988 through 1999, and prior to that led the Executive Development Center at Santa Clara University (1981–1987). Jim founded the Joint Center for Human Services Development at San Jose State University (1972–1980) and was on the staff of the School of Social Work, University of Texas. His career in training and development began in 1969 when he conducted seminars for Community Action Agency staff and volunteers in the war on poverty effort. Following graduation from Michigan State University (B.A. with honors in political science), he served as a Peace Corps volunteer (1967–1969). Jim also received a certificate from San Jose State University's

School of Business for completion of the internship in organization development. Jim can be reached at jim@kouzes.com.

Barry Posner is professor of leadership at Santa Clara University (Silicon Valley, California), where he has received numerous teaching and innovation awards and served as dean of the Leavey School of Business for twelve years (1996–2009). An internationally renowned scholar and educator, Barry is author or co-author of more than a hundred research and practitioner-focused articles. He currently serves on the editorial review boards for *Leadership and Organizational Development, Leadership Review,* and *The International Journal of Servant-Leadership.* Barry is a warm and engaging conference speaker and dynamic workshop facilitator. Barry received his baccalaureate degree with honors from the University of California, Santa Barbara, in political science; his master's degree from The Ohio State University in public administration; and his doctoral degree from the University of Massachusetts, Amherst, in organizational behavior and administrative theory. Having consulted with a wide variety of public and private sector organizations around the globe, Barry currently sits on the board of director of EMQ Family First. He has served previously on the board of the American Institute of Architects (AIA), Junior Achievement of Silicon Valley and Monterey Bay, San Jose Repertory Theater, Public Allies, Big Brothers/Big Sisters of Santa Clara County, the Center for Excellence in Nonprofits, Sigma Phi Epsilon Fraternity, and several start-up companies. Barry can be reached at bposner@scu.edu.

Mark Morrow is a freelance book editor and writer specializing in the areas of workplace learning, organization development, human resources, and general business. Most recently he served as the manager of acquisition and author relations at ASTD Press (the American Society for Training & Development's book publishing division).

Prior to joining ASTD Press, he was an executive editor at McGraw-Hill's professional book publishing division. His reporting and journalism experience includes daily newspapers, trade and professional newsletters and magazines, as well as freelance photography for *People, Esquire,* and *Fortune,* and other national and regional magazines and newspapers. His book of photographs and personal essays, *Images of the Southern Writer,* featured more than fifty southern-born authors, including Tennessee Williams, Eudora Welty, Robert Penn Warren, William Styron, Walker Percy, and Cormac McCarthy.

Notes

Notes